SHENANIGANS
S E R I E S

FOSTER & THAT BAD, B.A.D.D. BULLY

Jil Ross

Illustrated by Gwendolyn Pruitt

EbonyEnergy Publishing

Foster & That Bad, B.A.D.D. Bully – The Shenanigans Series

Second edition 2010

Author photo by Walter Mitchell

Book design Zahidulsajib
Editing by Rebecca Hayes

Published in the United States by EbonyEnergy Publishing
Imprint of Highest Good Publications
P.O. Box 43476
Chicago, IL 60643-0476

ISBN-10: 1-59825-945-8
ISBN-13: 978-1-59825-945-2

Library of Congress Control Number 2009928189

Books by Jil Ross

Foster & That Bad, B.A.D.D. Bully

Marie Plays Homeless

Foster the Mummy

The Real Nitty Gritty

The Blake Family Vacation

What's the Matter Mr. Ticklebritches?

Visit the author's website!

http://shenaniganseries.com

Dedicated to
Julian and Elliott

And in the memory of Dr. Rory Donnelly, who was an advocate of
change, unity and understanding

The Shenanigans Series™ Story

I created the Shenanigans Series™ as a result of not being able to find 'relevant,' challenging and thought-provoking books for my two children to read when they became interested in reading chapter books. While some children have become bored with the lack of viable reading choices; the stories of the Shenanigans Series™ offer stimulating storylines that are humorous and entertaining, yet grounded in moral lessons and require its readers to take self-evaluation.

In addition I had concerns with statistics that revealed how some children in urban areas had discouragingly low reading scores. Since that time my mission and commitment has been to be an instrument in getting young readers excited about reading and motivated to read.

All of the stories that I write are inspired by true events. The stories are told with humor and are grounded with moral foundations that provide practical lessons. Books in the series discuss issues such as: bullying, poverty, homelessness, theft, fire safety, first-aid, family values, the art of negotiation, critical thinking, self-regulation and self-evaluation. Each book includes a spelling guide and questions for thought and discussion, or written responses, a tool that educators and parents that home school appreciate.

...Reading Is a Form of Entertainment!!

Jil M. Ross

Words to Look for & Their Meaning

BULLY

Pronounced: **bul**-ly

(noun) some one who is cruel to smaller and weaker people

CHUMMY

Pronounced: **chum**-mee

(adjective) having a relationship of friends or close pals

EXASPERATING

Pronounced: ig-**zas**-per-ate

(verb) to irritate or provoke, to annoy extremely

WEASEL

Pronounced: **wee**-zul (noun) a sneaky person

STENCH

Pronounced: stench

(noun) a strong stinky, bad, foul odor

SCOFF

Pronounced: skof (verb) to mock or scorn

NONCHALANT

Pronounced: **non**-sha-**lant**

(adjective) cool, unconcerned, unexcited

GRIMACE

Pronounced: **grim**-ace

(noun) a facial expression of pain, contempt or disgust

GANGLY

Pronounced: **gang**-lee

(adjective) tall and thin, long and slender

INSTIGATE

Pronoun: **in**-ste-gate

(verb) to urge, encourage or provoke an action

DEVILMENT

Pronounced: **de**-vil-ment

(noun) a devilish action or conduct

ECSTATIC

Pronounced: ec-**stat**-tic

(adjective) the feeling of great delight

DESPISE

Pronounced: de- **spise**

(verb) to regard with distaste or disgust

SEETHING

Pronounced: **seeth**-ing

(verb) to be in a state of excitement or agitation (noun) the act of being excited or agitated

CHUMP

Pronounced: chump (noun) a stupid person

ACCOMPLICE

Pronounced: uh-**kom**-plis

(noun) a person who helps a lawbreaker or criminal

SUCKER PUNCH

Pronounced: **suck**-er-punch

(verb) to strike someone with an unexpected blow

CHAPTER 1

Have you ever had something happen to you – and if it had not happened to "*YOU,*" then you would have never believed it *ever* happened at all? Well, that's exactly how I've been feeling for a few weeks now. It all started around the time spring break was about to begin. Maybe I should start from the beginning…

*****

Bilbo Philpot had been my locker mate for the entire school year and he was a real slob. The lockers

in school are very small and he refused to keep his side of it clean. His papers were all over; there was mud on his baseball cleats and on his winter boots that he should have taken home months ago. He stuck his chewed gum on the inside of the locker and left his old lunch over weekends and long holidays. Some of my classmates complained that they could smell one of his old rotten meat sandwiches up and down the hallway. Boy was he nasty!

The door of the locker couldn't even close all the way, because it was bursting with so much junk; it was so overloaded that when I did open it, lots of stuff fell straight to the floor.

I was ecstatic when Mrs. Princeton, my homeroom teacher, announced that Bilbo Philpot and his family were moving out of town over spring break and that he would be transferring to a different school.

Our spring break began on a Friday, and Bilbo's last day was the Thursday before. On Friday of that week, I stayed after school for two hours, cleaning out the locker. From home, I'd brought a pail, rag, scrub brush, sponge, a scraper, plastic gloves, liquid cleansers, and I borrowed my dad's hand-held vacuum

– I was serious!

I knew that cleaning this locker was going to take a lot of work. I had to wash it out, scrub it down, sanitize it and spray it. I had to vacuum the corners of the locker to get small bits and pieces of crackers and crumbled-up potato chips out of it, throw away his old, musty soccer outfit, his smelly gym shoes, and an old carton of orange juice that had swollen up from the acid and the heat. It looked like it would explode at any second.

I even had to spray the locker with bug spray to kill the gnats that had been living in an old, wet, brown

paper bag that had rotten fruit and a moldy peanut butter and jelly sandwich in it.

After I finished washing the locker with three different cleansers, I dried it out. Once it was dry, I hung an extra strong air refresher in it, like the one my mother puts in my hamper to kill the stench of my dirty baseball uniform.

I knew it would probably take the entire ten days of spring break to make the locker smell fresh again. Once I hung an air freshener on a hook in the locker, I slammed the locker door and didn't look back.

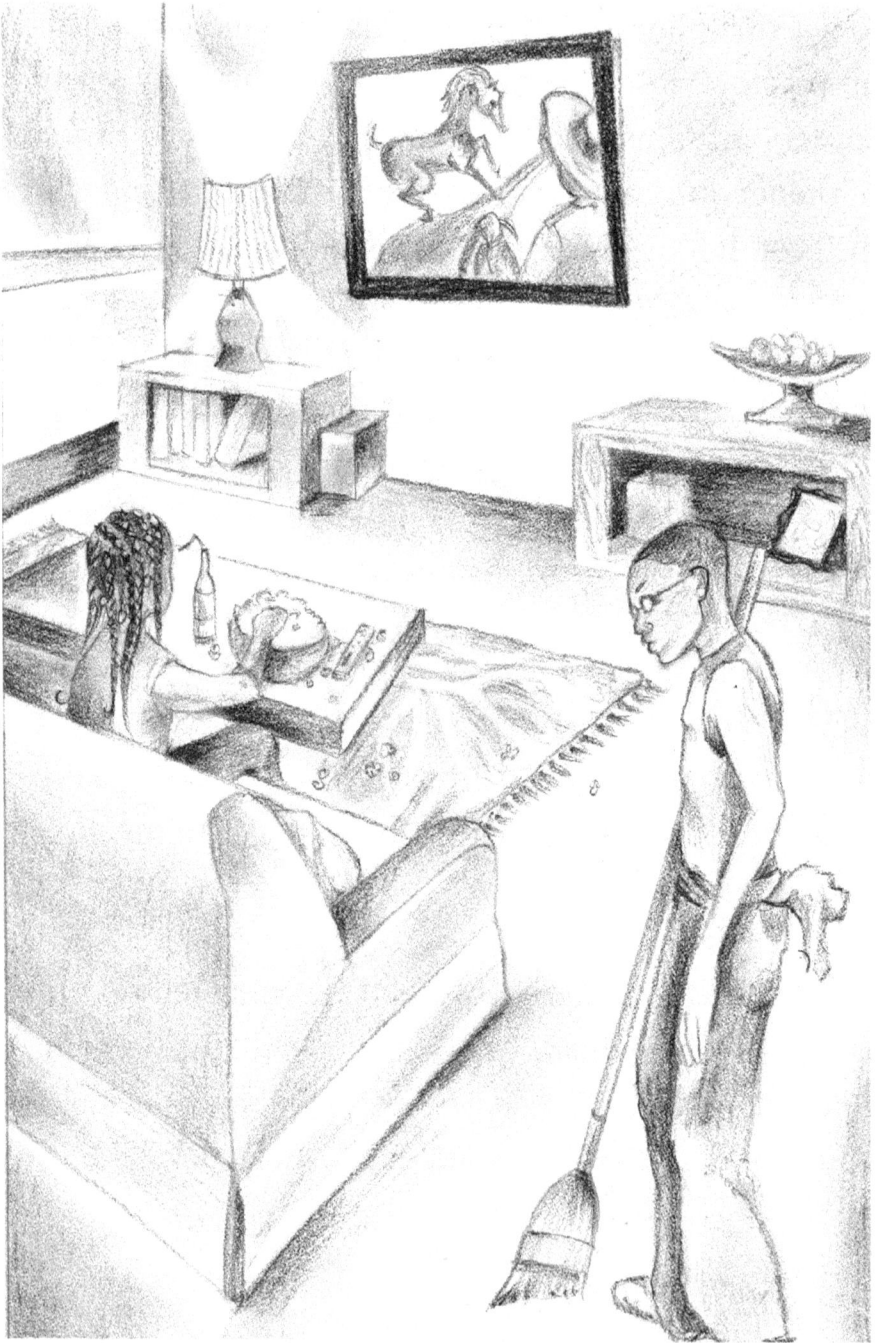

CHAPTER 2

The ten days of spring break flew by. My mother decided that rather than take a vacation, she wanted us to spend time cleaning around the house. This meant that it would definitely be no vacation for Marie and I, *but especially me.* I say this because when my mother gets in cleaning mode, *watch out!* There is no stopping her. Why, I even heard my dad mumble that he was glad to be going to work. He knew full well what Marie and I were in for.

Cleaning out my school locker had wiped me out and that's just a small locker. My mother was talking about cleaning the entire house, and I understood completely that meant the majority of the work would fall on me. It's a well known fact that every time Marie wants to get out of doing something, *which is most of the time,* she'll come up with some fictitious ailment; claim to not feel good, or have a headache, or that she hurt her hand or stubbed her toe, or broke a fingernail, or *something*, or *anything* or *everything*! The girl is useless!

It's unbelievable to me that my mother hasn't seen through Marie's drama. What's worse is that I always end up having to do everything that Marie *claims* she can't do. It doesn't help that when I try to expose Marie's antics, my mother scolds me. It's just not *fair*!

******

When I walked into the kitchen, I saw Marie sitting there at the kitchen table with the first aid kit,

claiming to have cut her finger. I walked over and took a closer look. "Mommy, this is not a cut, it's a scratch – and an old one at that! That's the same scratch she had last week when you asked her to take out the garbage and she claimed to be cut."

I pleaded with my mother to see past Marie's fake crisis. Mom just ignored me, as usual. I was seething mad as I looked at Marie sitting at the table, smiling as she unraveled a roll of bandage and dipped cotton balls in alcohol until they were drenched and soggy, nursing an invisible cut. To top it off, she put so much greasy ointment on her finger that the bandage wouldn't stick, and then she started the entire process all over again. She was just wasting time, again, and getting away with it, again.

My mother must have known that I was about to blow my top, because, before I could say a word, she snapped at me and said, "Foster, stop bellyaching and get moving. You're wasting time talking when you

could be working!" "Yes Ma'am," I said and grudgingly did as I was told.

I figured that I would just clean whatever I thought needed to be cleaned; but my mother had a different idea. She handed me three lists of things I had to do, things that I was responsible for cleaning. When I read the list my head almost spun around. "It's going to take longer than the days of my spring break to do all this," I complained. The list read:

List I – <u>your bedroom</u>

1. Clean your closet. Put all of the clothes that don't fit into a bag to be donated

2. Clean off your bookshelf and put the books that you no longer read in a box to be donated

3. Throw away all the junk, broken toys and candy wrappers that are underneath your bed

4. Sweep and mop the floor in your bedroom and your closet

5. Wash the walls down

6. Clean the insides of your windows and the mirror

7. Empty your trash pail

After completing list 1, I was to go into the basement and;

List II – the basement

1. Change all the mop heads

2. Clean the grease trap

3. Clean the lint trap from the furnace and the dryer

4. Clean your old toy chest. Put the toys that are in good condition in a bag to donate; put the others that are broken or missing pieces in the trash

5. Take the trash out Finally…

List III – the yard and garage

1. Clean out the space where your bike, skate-boards, unicycle and sports equipment is kept

2. Move all the old junk and furniture out to the street to be picked up by the garbage truck

3. Sweep the garage floor; make sure to sweep out the spider webs

4. Hose down the garage floor

5. Get the leaf blower and blow all the leaves from the front and back yard

6. Rake them up, bag them and put them out near the garbage pails

That's ALL – You're Done!

"Is she joking…? I'll be dead before I'm done," I scoffed. "What does Marie have to do?"

"For your information, I have to match the socks in the laundry bag that got separated from their mates, I have to dust and I have to clean all of the windows and mirrors, in the entire house with glass cleaner, except for your bedroom. I also have to clean out the stove," Marie said.

She tried to make it seem she had lots of work to do, but we both knew that it really wasn't a lot. She thought that if she talked slow and seemed exhausted and overwhelmed that I would think she'd be working as hard as I, but I knew better. In fact, she was going to be able to sit and watch television while she mated the socks. The more I thought about it, the angrier I became. Marie, *the slickster*, tried to make it seem like her chores were long and difficult but I saw past her trickery.

I was able to complete all of list one and part of list two on the first day of break. The grease trap was the worst! It was messy. The rod got stuck and when I yanked on it too hard, it flung out and grease was all over me and the basement floor and wall, which resulted in me having to wash down the walls, plus

mop three times over to get the mess up and then re- clean the mop heads.

By then I was both dirty and tired. As I walked pass the family room on my way outside to rinse the mop heads with the water hose, I heard Marie laughing. I peeked into the family room to see what was so funny - just to find her sitting on the sofa, watching cartoons on television with her feet propped up and her hand in a bowl of microwave popcorn.

I thought to myself, *"I despise Marie."* I know it was not a nice thought, but I was upset that she did not once offer to get off that couch and help me. She had to have heard me yell when I was falling from sliding on the grease or the sound of clanging from the rod and mop and pail as they hit the wall. But did she even so much as holler down to me in the basement to see if I was okay or if I needed help? No. *"She'll get hers,"* I thought.

I was so annoyed with Marie that I stopped talking to her hours earlier. She had completed all of her chores within a couple of hours whereas mine had taken all day and I was not even close to being finished. My mother tried to convince me that Marie's list 'seemed' shorter, because she did not have to clean her bedroom since she keeps it clean most of the time, anyway. I still had nothing to say to Marie, with her fake hurt finger. It was no surprise to me that no sooner than her short list of chores was complete, she took the bandage off her finger, which had magically healed. She never ceases to amaze me.

Once the mop was cleaned, I heard my mother say, "Foster come on in and eat dinner." Boy, was I glad. I figured if I started early the next morning that I would be finished with the garage and yard work by 3:00PM and would have a chance to ride my bike over to Kevin's house, and then we would go to the park and meet with Adam and Lafi and some other friends for a game of baseball.

But for now all I wanted to do was sit down and eat dinner, take a shower and then go to bed. I was wiped out.

CHAPTER 3

I guess I was more tired than I realized, because when I awoke the following morning, it was 11:00AM, and I hardly ever slept that late. I jumped out of bed, put on my clothes and rushed to complete my chores. I didn't even stop to brush my teeth. I wanted to hurry and finish the rest of list two and knock out list three, because I knew that my friends would be calling in the afternoon to ask if I could meet them at the park. I didn't want to risk asking my mother if I could go and hear her tell me "NO," because my chores were not complete.

Which reminds me, my grandmother always says, "Do what you have to do, so that when the time comes, you can do what you want to do."

My mother was at the stove and I smelled breakfast sausage, toast and potatoes cooking, but I did not bother stopping to eat. I heard the phone ringing and my mother starting to say, "Foster, would please answer the…" but I flew past her and by the time she completed her sentence, I was already in the basement. Marie must have still been asleep. I did not see her and I did not hear her, but I also wasn't looking for her as I ran through the kitchen. I was on a mission. I was determined not to be cooped up in the house cleaning for my entire spring break. I wanted to have some fun with my friends.

I had just finished sorting my toys; putting some away, throwing some away and putting others in a bag to donate. I took one final look at the basement to make sure it was clean to my mothers' standards, picked up the two bags of trash and headed outside.

I had just gotten the leaf blower out and was about to start it up when I saw my mother come outside and walk towards me. *Oh no, what does she want me to do now?* I thought to myself... *But I said,* "Hey, Mom, what's going on?" I asked hesitantly.

She winked at me, smiled and said, "Foster, just to let you know that there's a great reward that awaits you once you're all done."

"Ooh! What?" Marie asked. She seemed to have appeared out of nowhere.

"Mom isn't talking to you!" I snapped.

Marie folded her arms and rolled her eyes at me.

"One of my clients just called. He was so happy with the job I did on the commercial for Caldwell's Dry Cleaning that he gave me these," she said and waived four tickets in the air.

"What are they for?" I asked.

"Yeah, what are they for?" Marie repeated. "They are four tickets for the grand opening of The Maxx Extreme Sports Park!" she said.

"Wow, when are we going?" Marie asked before I could even open my mouth.

"*We're* not going," she said, "I am giving all four tickets to Foster so that he can take three of his friends. It's for tomorrow night."

"Really, Mom, really?" I was flabbergasted. I was so happy, I danced with the leaf blower and jumped for joy. I even laughed out loud when I the saw the disappointed look in Marie's crusty little eyes. *Serves her right...*

I love extreme sports: auto racing, moto-cross, super-cross, enduro-forestry, dirt track, arena-cross, hare scrambles, drag racing, hill climbing and skateboarding, I love it all! She showed me the brochure of the event, and it said that my favorite motocross competitor, James Stewart, was going to be there, live and in person. When I read this I became ecstatic! In fact, I didn't complain about my chores anymore. I think I even worked a little faster and harder.

Finally, by 4:00PM, I was done. All three lists were complete. I grabbed my baseball cap, bat and glove, got my on my bike and headed to Kevin's house. Kevin and I rode our bikes to the park, where we met up with

Lafi and Adam. After we played baseball with some other kids at the park, the four us sat underneath a tree and talked.

Kevin, Lafi, Adam and I live in the same neighborhood, but only Kevin and I live on the same block, although we attend different schools. Lafi and I have been friends the longest, ever since kindergarten. Adam and I are friends from church and scouts. And even though only Lafi, Adam and I attend the same school, all three of them are my closest friends. I asked the three of them if they'd like to go with me to The Maxx Extreme Sports Park.

"Awesome!" exclaimed Lafi. "So cool!" said Adam

"Are you serious? Are you serious?" Kevin kept repeating as he jumped up and gave all of us a high-five.

They were even more excited when I told them that we got meal tickets, too, and that no grown-ups would be hanging around. It was going to be just us four. I could not wait for the next night to roll around.

CHAPTER 4

After my mother picked-up each of my friends, we were driving along and talking in the car. First, we talked about the homework we were given over spring break, and then we started talking about our favorite athletes and wrestlers and who we each thought was the best, the worst, the fastest and the toughest, who was good and who was bad.

That's when Kevin interrupted and said, "If you all want to talk about who is real bad then I have a story for you… There's this kid in my class… well, he *was* in my class. He's so bad that he's the reason we got tons of homework over spring break."

"What does one student misbehaving in class have to do with your teacher assigning homework to the entire class?" my mother asked curiously.

"The boys name is Barlow, but our class nick-named him 'B.A.D.D,' because he caused so many problems in class that our teacher could not teach," Kevin replied.

"What do you mean?" Adam asked.

"Go ahead, we're listening," I added, speaking for the group.

"Okay, here's what happened…" Kevin told the story…

"Our class decided we wanted to have a classroom party at the end of the school year. Our teacher told us that she thought it would be a good idea for the class to save money for the party, instead of asking our parents for the money."

"That was a *great* idea," my mother commented. "To raise the money, our homeroom teacher,

Mrs. Duckwally, suggested we bring in our loose change, you know, pennies, nickels, dimes and quarters. We put the change in a glass piggybank that she kept on her desk. All the students in my class started bringing in change right after we got back from the Martin Luther King Holiday weekend. The class agreed that four months would be enough time to save the money.

We had to figure out how much money we needed to have a party; the cost of pizza, plates, napkins, cake, soda, snacks, balloons, everything. The class did research and calculated that $75.00 would be enough. Everyday, we would drop money into the piggybank. Mrs. Duckwally counted the money each Friday during lunch, and then let the class do a math problem to figure out how far away we were from our goal. Well, last Friday, Mrs. Duckwally reported that our class had saved more than enough money. We had saved $89.00 in only two months! The whole class was really excited."

"Wow, that's a lot of money. I could buy three disks for my game-box with that," Adam said.

"I could buy a lot of baseball cards, CDs and candy with that kind of money," I added.

"Let him finish the story," Lafi said, agitated that we had interrupted.

Kevin continued, "B.A.D.D had been getting in trouble in class all week long. He had been acting out and making noises every time Mrs. Duckwally turned her back to write on the chalkboard.

On Monday he tied Lance Keppler's shoestrings together and when Lance got up to sharpen his pencil, he fell on the floor and accidentally bit his tongue. He had to go to the nurse's office, because he was bleeding so badly. Tuesday, he put a tack in Christy Green's chair and when she sat down the pain she felt caused her to scream. Wednesday, each time Mrs. Duckwally turned to write on the board, he quacked like a duck to make fun of her name, and Thursday, when Emilio was closing the window to stop the rain from coming into the classroom, B.A.D.D yanked on the window causing Emilio to smash his fingers."

"Why didn't the teacher punish him?" my mother asked.

"Mrs. Duckwally couldn't ever catch him doing anything wrong, not once. She had a pretty good idea who was causing the problems. But she just couldn't catch him."

"Why wouldn't Christy or Lance or Emilio tell on him?"

"They were afraid to snitch on him. Snitches are not cool in our school."

"Why not?" I asked

"Because the last kid who snitched on Barlow ended up with a black-eye," Kevin told us.

"Wow, that kid is *bad*!" Adam said

"Let him finish the story, you guys!" Lafi insisted. He was intrigued.

"Okay, okay… Like I said, right after lunch, Mrs. Duckwally announced that our class had saved $89.00.

Then B.A.D.D asked permission to go to the washroom. A few seconds after he left the classroom, the fire alarm went off and the principal made an announcement that everyone had to exit the building immediately. No one knew why the alarm had gone off, because there was no smoke. We assumed it was a practice drill.

When everyone was outside, each teacher took attendance to make sure that everyone was out of the building safely. The only student missing in the *entire* school was Barlow. The Fire Marshall had to come and reset the school alarm system. Once the fire Marshall gave his okay, we went back inside. When we walked back in our classroom, all the people in my class, including Mrs. Duckwally, stopped in their tracks. Someone had broken the glass piggybank, and all the money was gone. All of it! The entire class turned to look at Barlow."

"No Way! You're kidding!" I said.

Adam, Lafi, my mother and I sat quietly, listening as this story unfolded.

Kevin continued, "When we all looked at him, he just shrugged his shoulders and said that he didn't know what had happened, but no one believed him. We knew he had broken the bank and stolen the money. The window of the classroom had been opened and the wind was blowing papers everywhere. My teacher asked me to run and get the janitor so that he could sweep the mess of glass and papers that were all over the floor.

"Barlow, where were you during the fire alarm? And what happened in this classroom while we were outside?" Mrs. Duckwally insisted.

"I don't know," he replied. He looked her right in the eye.

"'Barlow, I want to know what happened to the piggybank and I want you to tell me now!'" she demanded.

And with a sly smile on his face, he answered her, "'I said, 'I don't know.'" All the students' heads were going back and forth, looking at Mrs. Duckwally and Barlow, Mrs. Duckwally and Barlow; it was as if we were looking at a tennis match.

"'Why is the window open?'"

"'I'm not sure. I thought you or someone else in the room opened it,'" he said with a grin... showing that chipped tooth of his.

"'Where were you while we were outside?'" Mrs.

Duckwally was beginning to get angry... I could tell.

"In a nonchalant tone Barlow said, 'I went to the bathroom... I heard the alarm go off, but my pants were pulled down. I couldn't just run into the hall with my pants pulled down, could I?'

"Some of the kids in my class snickered, but Mrs. Duckwally cut her eyes at them and they hushed. She did not think any of this was funny. Then Barlow went on to say, 'By the time I finished in the bathroom, the alarm had stopped and everyone was on their way back inside. When I heard voices and the sound of feet coming up the steps, I just came back to class and took my seat. I was just as surprised as you all were when I came back in the room and saw the broken piggybank. That's when I noticed the opened window.' *He was smiling now...*

"And then he said, 'In fact, now that I think about it, I think I saw somebody jumping out of the window. Maybe it was a robber… Yeah that's it! A robber took the money and then he jumped out the window to get away.'"

"Unbelievable!" Adam said.

Lafi, Adam my mother and I were shocked by this story. We sat there and listened as Kevin finished telling us what happened…

"This is the best part; Mrs. Duckwally called the principal down to the classroom to look at the mess. In front of the entire class, she asked Barlow to repeat the story – I could tell by the look on my principal's face that she did not believe him, either. He repeated the story, word for word.

"Mrs. Duckwally was upset, because once again, she had no proof that Barlow was behind this. Our principal was just as angry, especially since the entire school had evacuated the building because of a prank. Then the principal asked Barlow to come to the office so she could have a talk with him about what *he said* had happened.

"Now get this, when he got up from his chair, coins started dropping from his head to his feet; from his pants pockets, shirt pocket, balled up in his fists, down in his socks and shoes, underneath his baseball cap, everywhere. It was something to see. This dude had no shame." Kevin sat back in his seat and shook his head.

"Well, what happened to him?" Lafi asked, he was practically sitting at the edge of his seat.

"Oh, yeah, Barlow was kicked out of school. His mom had to come. They cleaned out his locker and desk, and he was out of there. But because he interrupted class all week, our class had lots of work to make up, which is why we had so much now over spring break."

"That story is very upsetting," my mother said. "It's a shame your teacher had to put up with his foolishness and with him bullying your classmates all year."

"Barlow hadn't been at my school all year; he had just transferred to our school two months ago *after* he got kicked out of his last school." Kevin explained.

"What school will he go to now?" I asked

"I don't know and I don't care!" said Kevin. "Things are back to normal in my class, now that he's gone, and we don't even talk about him."

"You're right, Kevin, that boy was bad," my mother said.

"He was bad to the bone," Kevin added

By the time Kevin finished his story, my mom was pulling into the parking lot of the sports arena. She pointed out the spot where she would pick us up and told us she would be back in three hours. She reminded us to stay together.

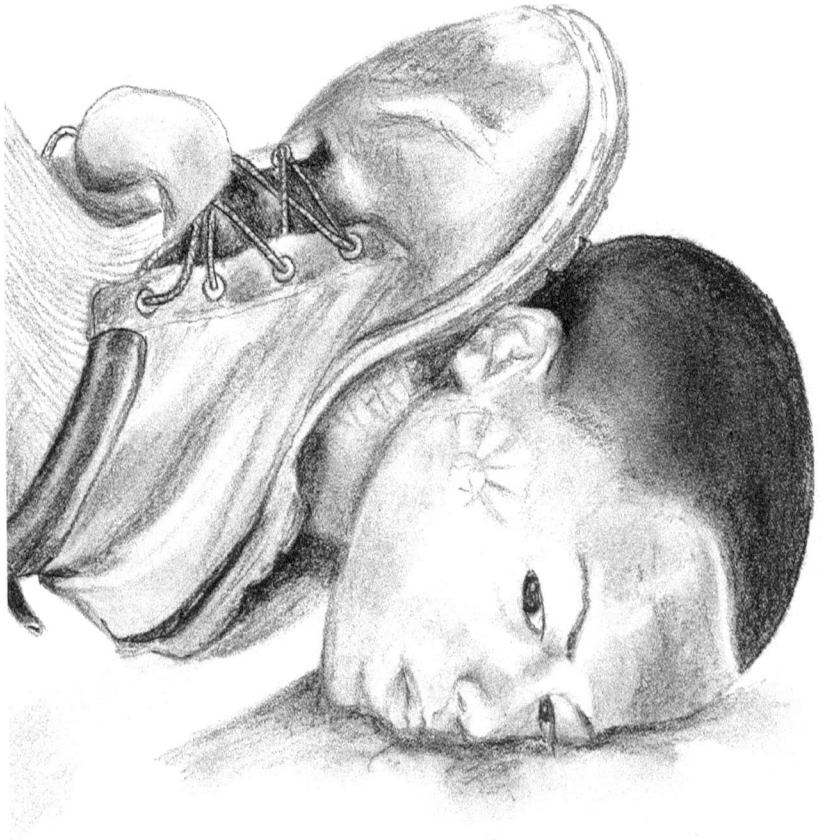

CHAPTER 5

The four us got out of the car and started walking towards the entrance. That's when Kevin realized he'd left his camera in my mom's car. "Aw, man, I think I left my camera in your mom's car," he panicked.

"She's still parked there, run back and catch her before she leaves, we'll wait for you at the door," I told Kevin as he took off running.

Adam, Lafi, and I were walking through the fence and towards the entrance when we heard someone say, "Pssst, over here. Come over here." We all stopped and looked around, but didn't see anything. We heard it again, "Psst, can you come over here? I need your help," we heard a voice say. We hesitated because we couldn't see anyone. It was pretty dark out. I could not clearly see a face; all I could see was a crooked smile and a chipped tooth.

I took a step closer to the fence to get a better look and then, BAM! Out of nowhere this chump sucker-punched me, knocking me to the ground! A big kid! A *huge* kid! He knocked me right to the ground! He put his foot on my head and snatched the tickets out of my hand.

Everything happened so quickly that when Adam and Lafi realized what was happening, I was already on the ground. The two of them tried to charge the big lug, but with one shove, he knocked them both down to the ground. This dude was stronger than me, Lafi, Kevin and Adam all put together. He was solid, like a big glob of clay. I kept thinking that if I didn't do something, this thug was going to use my ticket to get into the show. All of a sudden, with all my strength, I grabbed his ankle. His foot was now pressing down harder, smashing my face into the dirt.

I don't know what came over me. The more I thought of this guy stealing our tickets, the stronger I became. It seems that I got the strength of a super hero and I squeezed his ankle hard, with all my might, until his knee bent, then I reached up and punched him in the stomach, once he was down I punched him in the face, and then he fell over. As soon as I was certain that I'd knocked the wind out of him, I jumped up, dusted myself off, snatched the tickets back from him and me, Lafi and Adam took off running. By the time we got to the entrance we were all breathing hard.

"What just happened?" Lafi asked, in a bit of a daze.

"Yeah," Adam seconded, "what was that all about?"

I was still huffing and puffing and dusting my clothes off, but I responded, "Man, I don't know what was with that dude, but I was not about to let him take our tickets."

By then Kevin had gotten his camera and had caught up with us.

"I got my camera just in time; your mom was just about to pull out of the..." Before Kevin finished his sentence he took a second look at me, Lafi and Adam and said, "What happened to you guys," Kevin was puzzled. "You all look like you were in a fight. And Foster, why do you have a boot print on your face?"

Me, Lafi and Adam looked at each other.

"Let's go in, I will tell you about it later," I told him. I did not feel like talking about what had happened. I was not going to let that jerk ruin my evening.

*****

The evening was all that we thought it would be and more! We saw stunts, races and new ATVs and moto-cross bikes that were not going to be out until next year. We got a chance to take photos with famous motocross winners. The highlight of my night was when Kevin took a picture of James Stewart and me. He was really cool, just like he seems on television.

I was happy to see my friends were enjoying themselves as much as I was. Kevin and Lafi even took a picture with two of the models that were standing around posing for pictures, and Adam won a T-shirt when his ticket number was called during the raffle.

When the big event was about to begin on the track, we took our seats. Wow! We had box seats and were practically sitting on the track. When my mother said we had meal tickets, we thought we could only get hotdogs and French fries, but a waitress came to our box seats and told us we could order *anything* we wanted from the menu.

"Anything?" I asked her to be sure. "Anything," she confirmed.

"And it's free, right?" Lafi asked. "Absolutely free," once again she confirmed.

"This is awesome!" Kevin was thrilled. I was too excited about everything that was going on and I didn't have much of an appetite; so I ordered nachos with extra cheese and hot peppers. Adam ordered the double deluxe chili-cheese dogs, an order of curly fries and chocolate pudding. Lafi wanted fried shrimp and French fries, and he ordered strawberry shortcake for desert. Kevin ordered a salad, onion rings and a steak!

We all laughed, because when the waitress delivered the steak, it was so big that it was hanging off of Kevin's plate. There was no way he'd be able to eat it all. We all ordered two sodas each. It was sneaky, we know, because if my mom, or if any of our moms were there, they would not have allowed us to order one soda, let alone two. But since there were no adults around, we all said, "Go for it!"

Soon, the lights went down and the extreme sports show began while we ate. Kevin took plenty of pictures. We saw lots of extreme stunts and willies that the announcer warned "Please DO NOT try this at home!" This was one of the best times of my life.

With all the excitement, pictures, food and good times, I had forgotten all about what had happened earlier, with that grump. We were all pretty exhausted by the end of the night. My friends all gave me a high-five and said, "thank you," as they each were dropped off at home. Kevin promised to give each of us a set of pictures soon.

I thanked my mom again for giving me the tickets to share with my friends. I fell asleep that night with a big smile on my face.

The rest of the week went by pretty quickly. I walked to the library and borrowed some books to read.

One day our grandma took Marie, my cousin Jahari and me to the zoo. Then on the next day, my aunt Jori took us all to a movie. Before we knew it, spring break was over and it was time to return to school.

BOOK II

And then the trouble began...

CHAPTER 6

I was beginning to get bored at home so I was glad to be going back to school. Besides, my classroom was going to begin working on history projects the week we returned to school, which I was looking forward to. Our assignment included having to make a model of a famous American historical building and write a paper on the architect who designed it.

I had taken books out of the library on the subject and had a pretty good idea of what building I wanted to model. I hoped that my teacher would let us choose our project partners, because I wanted to work with Sammy Cheung. He made an awesome model airplane for the science fair and came in second place. I knew he would work as hard as I, and together we could come up with an award-winning project. Sammy, like me, is no slacker. I was also looking forward to **not** having a locker mate.

Dad dropped Marie and I off on his way to work. I found Lafi and Adam at the playground and we talked until the bell rang, but as soon as it did, I rushed inside. As we entered the school door, Adam remembered that he'd left his lunch on the playground. He ran out to get it and told me he'd see me in homeroom. Lafi has homeroom across the hall from us.

I walked fast, because I was curious to see how the locker turned out, I hoped that the horrible smell was gone. Last night, Kevin brought over the pictures from the night we had gone to the extreme sports event and I had a picture of me and James Stewart, and a photo of me, Lafi, Adam and Kevin that I wanted to hang in my locker before the first bell.

I opened my locker and to my surprise it was full. An unfamiliar jacket, baseball cap and different pair of muddy gym shoes were in it. There were magazine pictures of pit-bull dogs, Rottweiler dogs and pictures of wrestlers and cage fighters taped to the inside of the locker. In fact, the pictures took up the entire area of inside locker door. The locker was full, stuffed, all over again.

"What the heck is this?" I closed the locker to check the locker number and make sure I'd opened the right one... "Yeah, this is locker number 13..."

I scratched my head "What's going on?" I wondered. "Whose stuff is this?" I asked myself, out loud. I scratched my head some more but I couldn't figure it out. I stuffed my lunch into a tiny space I found on the top shelf of the locker. The only thing I could figure out was that maybe someone thought the locker was not being used, because it was empty and so clean, and decided to move in.

I had to let Mrs. Princeton know what was going on so that she could let the imposter know that this was *my* locker. I dashed into my homeroom to tell my teacher what was going on. I also hoped that Bilbo Philpot had not returned. Mrs. Princeton was at her desk talking to someone I didn't recognize.

"Mrs. Princeton, Mrs. Princeton," I called out to her. I did not realize that I was interrupting her conversation. As I got closer to Mrs. Princeton's desk, I saw that she was talking to a boy that I'd never seen before.

"Foster Blake," she replied sharply, "You know the rules of my classroom… You say excuse me when you see that I am speaking with someone. Show that you have good manners."

"Excuse me, Mrs. Princeton, but someone's stuff is in my locker."

"Yes, you are correct. There are someone's things in your locker. We have a new student joining our class. Foster Blake, meet your new locker partner, Barlow Aldwin Derrick Darden."

"What! I can't believe this. This is the most rotten luck! I spent two hours cleaning out my locker and I have a new locker partner." Unbelievable," I was thinking to myself.

Mrs. Princeton snapped her finger in my face. "Snap out of it, Foster," she raised her voice. "Do you hear me talking to you? I just introduced you to your new locker partner. Now I will leave you two alone to get to know each other better." Then she turned and walked away.

I extended my hand to offer him a handshake as a welcoming gesture, but he just looked down at my hand and did not shake it. Instead, he turned and walked away and sat in Adam's seat. Adam's desk was located in the back of the classroom; he was one of the few students in class that did not wear glasses and could easily see the blackboard from the back of the room.

"Hey, that seat belongs to Adam," I tried to tell him, but he just sat down anyway. I repeated myself, "I said that seat belongs to Adam." The guy just turned and starred at me with a blank look on his face.

Although I did not recognize him, there was something eerily familiar about him. I just could not put my figure on it.

Just as I got this feeling, the new kid went inside Adam's desk and took all of his belongings out, and sat them on top. *What's he doing? Putting Adam out of his desk?* I wondered...

Mrs. Princeton said to me, "Foster please take your seat, I am about to take attendance."

"But..."

As usual, she cut my words off. "Now!" she scorned. "Take your seat now and hold your comments until after attendance and announcements."

Quickly I went back to the locker and tried to find a space to hang my jacket and baseball cap. But my new locker partner had so much mud on his jacket and everything, that I just kept my things with me in class. It looked like he'd been rolling in mud or something. I even removed my lunch bag and decided to keep it in my desk. I slammed the locker and returned to the classroom.

I was angry. It was clear from that moment that the new boy, Barlow, and I were not going to be chummy. I did not know him but already I did not like him, at all.

The second bell rang just as Adam was making his way into the classroom. Adam walked over to his seat and found someone sitting at his desk with his stuff on top of it. "What's going on?"

"Who are you?"

Barlow just stared him up and down, but did not say a word.

Mrs. Princeton marched to the back of the room to see what the commotion was all about, "What seems to be the problem back here?" she asked.

Barlow replied. "There is no problem, ma'am. He was just telling me that since I am the new kid in class, he was going to let me have his seat, since I am near-sighted." Barlow wore a fake smile as he told this lie.

"What?" Adam said. "What?" I repeated.

"How noble of you, Adam, your kindness just earned you two extra credit points." Mrs. Princeton smiled, which is rare. "Gather your belongings and I will sit you up here, near me and the window." Adam looked back at him and grimaced. I looked over at him, too. I did not like this kid, not at all. Barlow looked at Adam and me and smiled a sly smile, and his chipped tooth was revealed.

Adam could care less about two extra credit points; he wanted his seat back.

"I know this brood from somewhere, but where?"
I wondered.

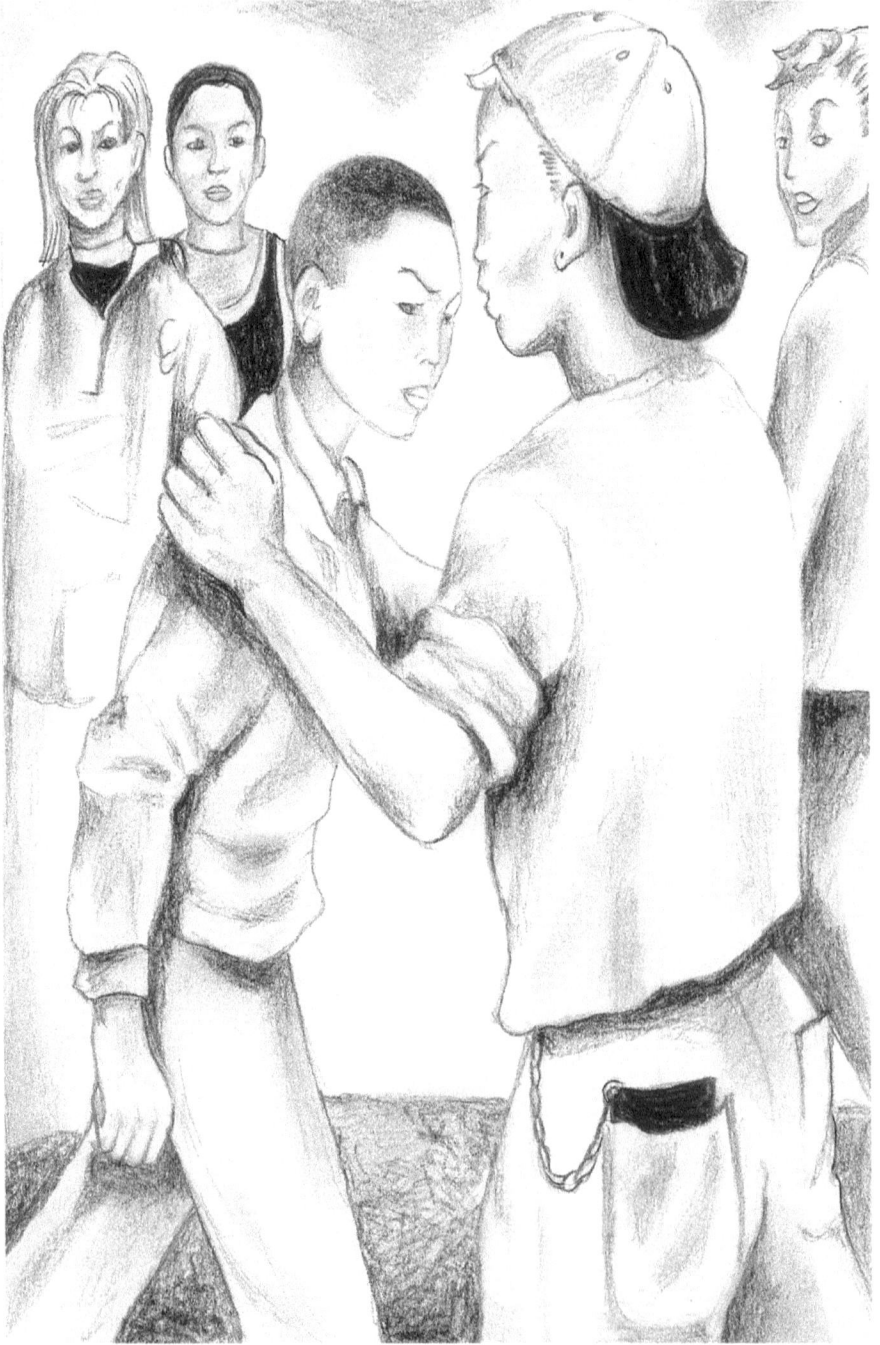

CHAPTER 7

"I think I've met him somewhere before, I just can't remember where," I told Lafi and Adam as we stood along the fence in the playground at recess.

"Well, I don't like him and he's a liar. My father always says that 'if a person is a liar, they are probably a thief, too,'" Lafi added.

"How do you know he's a liar, Lafi?" Adam wanted to know.

"Because he said that he was near-sighted. My uncle Yusuf is an Ophthalmologist, an eye doctor, and he once explained to me that *near-sighted* means that a person <u>cannot</u> see things from far away; and that *far-sighted* means that you <u>can</u> see things far away. They mean the opposite of what they seem... which means if Barlow was really near-sighted, he would need to sit in the front of the classroom to see the chalkboard."

"You're right, Lafi" I said, "I remember reading that before."

"I say we stay away from him. He sounds like bad news," Adam said.

"Yeah," Lafi and I agreed.

Just then Marie ran over to us and belted out, "Hey, I hear you all got a new boy in your class. Where is he?"

"Who knows and who cares?" Adam replied.

I could tell by the look on Marie's face that she was surprised by that response. She knew that in the past, Adam, Lafi and I always went out of our way to meet new students and make them feel welcome.

"Why do you say that?" Marie pried.

"He seems like trouble and we should keep our distance from him."

"So, it must be true, what I heard..." Marie said.
"What did you hear?" Lafi asked.

I shook my head at Marie, and warned, "Marie, you know what Mom and Dad told you about spreading rumors and gossiping..."

"Well, it seems that it may not be a rumor. It may be the truth. I heard that he was a liar and a thief and a bully." Marie gloated as she passed this information on.

"I knew it!" Adam belted out.

She continued, "A girl in my class knows someone, who is the cousin of someone, who is the neighbor of someone, who knows someone else who knows the new boy."

"What?" Lafi, Adam and I replied in unison.

Marie repeated, "A girl in my class knows someone... never mind. The bottom-line is that he has a reputation of not only being a liar and thief, but also a bully, and supposedly got kicked out of the last four schools that he attended. They also said he was caught stealing money."

"That's it!" I exclaimed. "The chipped tooth!" Then I turned to Lafi and Adam and said, "He's the boy from the Maxx Extreme Sport Park, in the parking lot. The one Kevin was telling us about... *remember?*" I winked, trying not to let on too much, since Marie was standing there.

"Yeah, that's the chump Foster was fighting with near the parking lot who tried to steal the tickets," Adam remembered.

"Ooh, I'm telling Mom, you were fighting." I could tell by the look on Marie's face that she was happy to have a piece of juicy detail to hang over my head.

"You'd better not. There was no fight. He tried to steal from me and I took back what was mine. Period. So don't go telling Mom and Dad. I don't want them worrying; I know how to handle myself." Then I gave Adam a dirty look for opening his mouth.

I was facing Marie, Adam and Lafi and noticed that they were pre-occupied looking at something going on behind me.

I turned to see what they were looking at. I could see a crowed headed our direction. Barlow was leading the crowd. Lafi, Adam, Marie and I wondered what was going on.

Before long, Barlow and a crowd of people were standing around us in a circle. Barlow walked up to me, Marie, Lafi and Adam and just stood there. He was with another boy who was from my classroom, named Xavier Peoples.

Xavier is a busybody. He is known for keeping up confusion and instigating. He will try and pal around with whoever is popular at the time. When Sammy Cheung won the state science fair, Xavier was his best friend; when Jada Ross was voted Snow Princess at the winter dance, he followed her around all the time; and when Justin DeWitt had his picture in the school paper for rescuing a cat, he was Justin's shadow.

The truth is that Xavier really has no friends. He is two-faced and is not really trusted by anyone in class. All the students know that he is not a loyal friend. He is only interested in a person based on how popular he or she is. It does not matter why a person is popular, only that they are popular. But even knowing this, I was surprised to see that, of all people, he was now Barlow's sidekick.

Barlow took a step closer to my face, raised his arms up and said, "What's up?"

I asked him back, "What's up?"

He took a step closer and said "You tell me what's up," he demanded.

"No, you tell me what's up? You're the one who walked over here and posed the question." By now we were walking slowly in a circle, shoulder to shoulder.

"What? You think you own the play ground?" He spat. Spit seeped from his chipped tooth. Barlow talked loud for the entire crowd to hear.

"What are you talking about?" I asked... *This is stupid and makes no sense. I was talking to my friends and my sister. How does this goof come up with the conclusion that I think I own the playground?* "What is this really about? I asked him.

"I heard that you said I stole from you..." He said, looking shifty and unsure of himself, as if he was putting up a front for the crowd of people.

"Yeah, Barlow heard you were telling people that he stole from you," said a voice in the crowd, and then Xavier peeked out his little head. He was attempting to egg them on, because he wanted to see a fight.

This made Marie angry. Xavier was getting on her nerves, and without thinking, she jumped in front of Xavier, pointed in his face and said to him, "Listen you little weasel, you need to shut-up and stop instigating. My brother didn't tell anyone that Barlow stole from him... What he said is that Barlow *tried* to steal from him, and he simply took back what was his." Then she thought about what she'd just said, looked at Foster and said, "Oops," as she covered her mouth.

The crowd started to get jumpy then, and I could tell they were there to see a brawl.

The truth was that Barlow did remember Foster and his friends from The Maxx Extreme Sports Park. He was angry that Foster and his friends had tickets to the event. They looked too happy that night and Barlow could not stand it. He was jealous and envious of them. Since Foster was holding the tickets that evening, he went after him and tried to take him down and take the tickets away.

The fact that Foster and his friends had gotten away with the tickets and had enjoyed themselves only made Barlow angrier. Now he had it in for Foster and he was determined to make his life miserable.

"So, you think I am trying to steal from you? If I wanted to steal from you I would not 'try'… I would just take it. You hear me?" Barlow said, as he took a step closer and got really, really close to my face.

"Yeah, you hear him?" Xavier repeated.

I balled my fist and looked him in the eye and said, "I'll tell you one thing. You'd better step off and step back." I was not playing.

"Or else what?" Barlow said, practically threatening me; "Or else what? You gonna tell on me? Are you a momma's boy?" He mocked me in a whining voice.

I did not reply. I just turned and attempted to walk away. I had gone to the playground to play and talk to my friends as I did everyday. I was not about to let this new kid, a bully, get the best of me. He was obviously looking for trouble and I was not going to give him the satisfaction of falling for his trap.

Then I felt a push from the back. I almost lost my footing and fell towards the ground, but I caught my fall and stood up straight.

The crowd was screaming that Barlow had done it, but I did not see him do it and I was determined to remain cool and not allow the crowed to get me worked up and into a frenzy.

In just the nick of time, I turned to look at Barlow. He was about to lunge at me and I jumped backwards out of the way, which caused him to fall on the ground. That really made him furious. He was about to swing at me when the bell rang and we had to return to school.

The crowd seemed disappointed that they had not seen a fight, which was a surprise to me. Our school is a good school and the people in my class are usually pretty quiet and like to study and mind their own business... except Xavier. They work hard and get good grades. It's amazing how one bad kid can bring out the worst of everybody! All of my classmates were acting like savages. I did not know these people.

My observation was disrupted when Barlow came up to me and threatened, "Expect IT when you least expect IT!" Then he walked into the school.

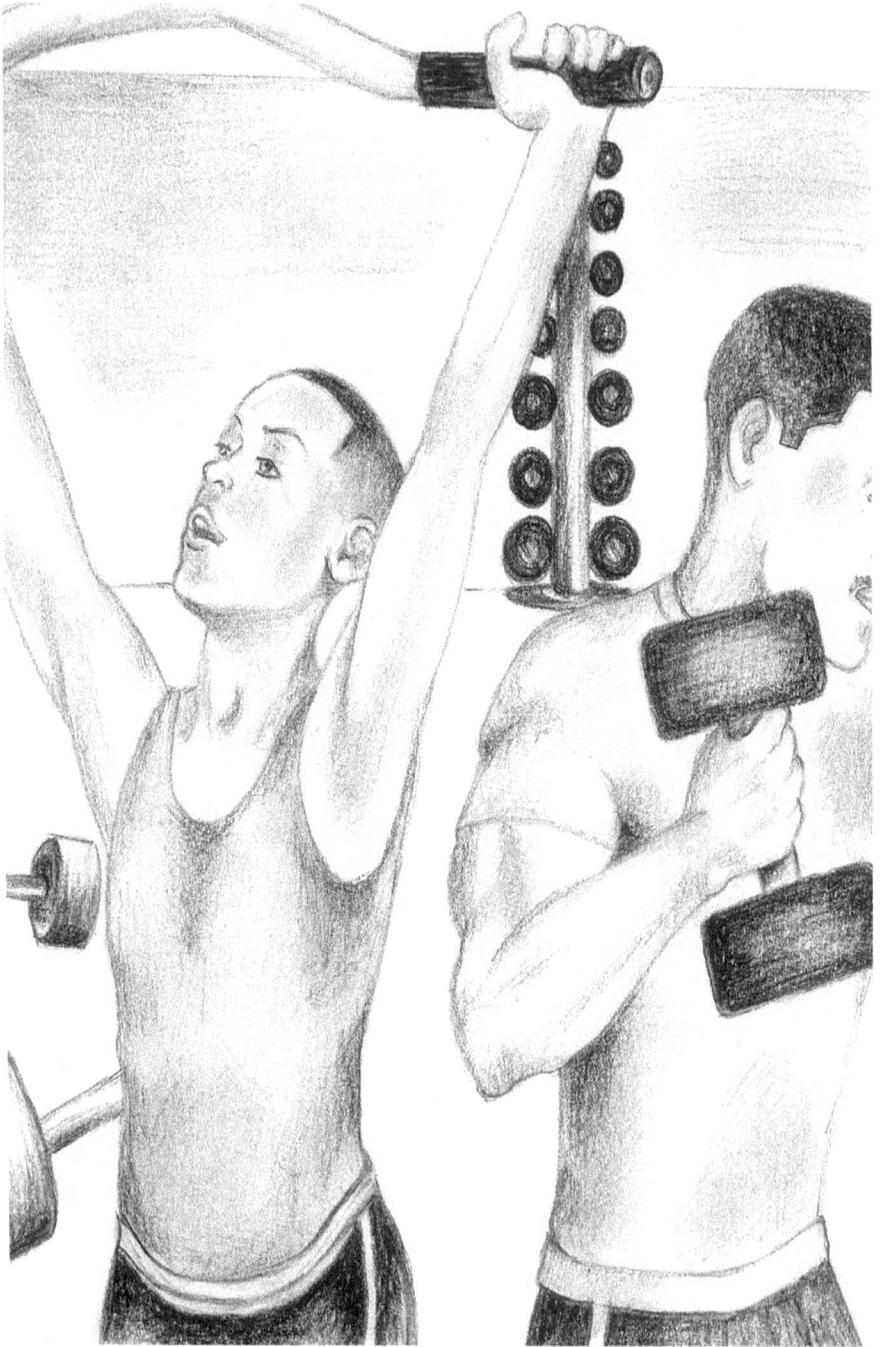

CHAPTER 8

The remainder of the school day was a blur... I could not figure out how I had gone from looking forward to being back at school to wondering how I was going to get through the remainder of the year with this bozo lurking around looking for a fight. I could not wait until the bell rung at the end of the school day; I had a headache and was ready to get home.

Lafi, Adam, Marie and I walked home together.

"Foster, man, what are you going to do? This kid has it in for you," Adam said. Then Lafi asked, "Do you think he recognized us from The Maxx Extreme Sports Park?"

"I don't know. It does not matter, anyway... I am going to mind my business, do my work and hopefully, the dude will chill out."

"I have a feeling he won't," Marie added, "I think you should just knock him out with the ole' *one- two jammy.*"

"What?" they all asked. They were surprised by Marie's remarks.

"You heard me... Kick him in the chicklettes!" Marie said as she kicked her leg to demonstrate what she was talking about.

Lafi and Adam laughed, but I thought about what my sister was saying. Maybe she was right, I didn't want my classmates to think I'm a punk and I that I would just sit by and let someone bully me.

Just then, we heard the sound of footsteps running behind us. Xavier was leading the group of students. He stopped when he caught up with me.

"What do you want, pipsqueak?" Marie got in his face, pointing her finger at him, again.

"What's up, Xavier?" I said.

"B.A.D.D. sent me to tell you that you and he have an appointment Friday after school, to fight out your differences... oops, I mean work out your differences."

"What are you talking about? And who is B.A.D.D?" Adam demanded.

"Barlow's nickname is B.A.D.D, which stands for Barlow Aldwin Derrick Darden... he's so bad, even his initials spell out the word B.A.D.D!" Xavier recited this as if it was some kind of honor or something.

"What do you mean, fight out our differences?" I asked. "Fight out what differences? I haven't talked to him enough to even have differences with him."

"Well, he said that you said that he tried to steal some tickets from you... and he did not like that."

"Although I never told anyone that, it is the truth. He did try to steal tickets from me, but he didn't succeed. Adam and Lafi were there when it happened. What is there to fight about? If you think about it, I should have more reason to want to fight him than he should want to have to fight me. They were my tickets."

"You do have a point," Xavier said, scratching his chin. "I don't really know. I am just delivering the message."

Lots of kids were standing around listening to this exchange. Xavier stood on a park bench and yelled out to the crowd. "FRIDAY AFTER SCHOOL, TELL LOTTIE, DOTTIE AND EVERYBODY! THERE IS GOING TO BE A FIGHT." Then Xavier took off running like a crazy jester, spreading the news to whoever would listen.

*****

"Foster, what are you going to do?" Marie asked in a panic. "You know that Mom and Dad don't want you fighting. And if your teacher finds out and tells the principal, they will suspend you, then you won't be able go to high school, which means that you won't be able to go to college then you'll end up being a bum on the street and…"

"Enough, Marie!" Adam, Lafi and I all said at the same time.

"First of all, there is no need for Mom and Dad to find out," I said, looking directly at Marie, as if to warn her to keep her mouth shut – which Marie has a hard time doing.

"You're right," Marie said, "just let him have it right between the eyes, and it will be over with, quick." Marie was worried for me. As much as she liked annoying me, she did not like it when someone else was picking on me, nor did she like the fact that Barlow was stirring-up trouble in our otherwise peaceful school.

Kevin had called and left a message on the answer machine, warning me that Barlow had transferred to my school and to beware. But by the time I got his message, I already knew.

I decided not to call Kevin back. I did not want to give this subject any more attention. I was tired of talking about it. I just wanted to complete my homework, eat dinner, and go into the basement and workout. I thought it would be smart to work on my strength before the big fight on Friday.

*****

"Where's your brother?" Mr. Blake, the children's father asked Marie.

"He's in the basement working out. He wants to be ready on Friday…"

"What's going on Friday?" Mr. Blake asked suspiciously.

"Uh-oh… What I mean is Wednesday. We are having an Olympic competition at school later this week and he just wants to be in shape." *Well that's*

kind of the truth since all of the gym classes were planning on having Olympic competitions, Marie thought to herself.

Their father went to the basement to check on Foster.

"Whoa, what's going on?" my father asked.

"Oh, I'm just getting a work-out," I said, trying to lift a 100 pound barbell over my head as I lay on my dad's weight bench.

"Foster, I think you need to remove some of these weights. You cannot start lifting weights at 100 pounds, especially on day one. You have to build your strength up to that level." He adjusted the weights to the right amount, so that I was able to lift them. My father and I tossed the medicine ball back and forth to each other. We did pull-ups, push-up and squats. After an hour of working out with my father, I was tired. "We're just getting warmed up," my father gloated. I waved good-bye and left the basement. I took a shower and went to bed.

CHAPTER 9

The next morning, I was so sore and stiff that I could hardly walk. I walked slowly into the kitchen to sit down and have breakfast with Marie before Dad dropped us off at school. As soon as I was able to comfortably sit in the chair, Marie said to me, "I'm concerned about you, Foster. You're too gangly to fight and have a real chance at winning. You should just karate-kick Barlow in the gonads and take off running while he's doubled over in pain."

I laughed at what Marie was saying, but not for long… My chest and stomach muscles were so sore

that I couldn't laugh too long or too hard. "Size has nothing to do with strength," I explained. We were about to leave for school when the phone rang. My mother answered the phone.

"Foster, that was Mr. Bobby. He wants you to stop by his barbershop after school. He says he will pay you to sweep the floor before he closes the shop."

"Cool," I like the idea of earning my own money. I also like to listen to the older men talk at the barbershop.

When I arrived at school, Adam offered that I could share the locker with him and Simon. Since our school lockers are small I knew it would tight, but there was no way I was going to share a locker with that dirty, lying thief. It took Bilbo Philpot seven months to dirty up our locker and it took Barlow only one day! I refused to clean-up someone else's mess, again.

During Tuesday announcements, Mrs. Princeton reminded the class to bring our gym clothes for the school Olympic Games tomorrow. Then she became serious and told us that the new art supplies for our class had come up missing. Someone had broken off the lock of the supply cabinet.

Later that day, it was reported that someone had used the missing paint and colored chalk to write graffiti and bad words on the walls of the washroom. Lafi, Adam and I knew who the culprit was, but had no proof.

Mrs. Princeton, my classmates and I were concerned about the theft. This was the first time we'd had a situation like this at our school.

Immediately after school, I headed to Mr. Bobby's Barbershop. I walked alone to the barbershop, while Lafi and Adam walked Marie home.

Once I crossed the street near the school, I heard a "Pssst" sound, just like the one I heard the night at The Maxx Extreme Sports Park. I was reading a book that I borrowed from the school library about Kung Fu fighting, and as I kicked my way down the street, I heard 'Pssst," again.

I looked up to see Barlow and Xavier, his sidekick, as they leaned on the light post. When I looked up, Barlow took his index finger and gestured slowly by moving it across this neck, like he was going to slit my throat by cutting me with a knife. That's when I took off my belt and tried to swing it about like I had seen done with chains in some Kung Fu fighting movies.

But then I accidentally smacked myself in the face with the belt buckle "Ouch!" – and so I put my belt back on my pants and made my way to the barbershop. I could hear Barlow and Xavier laughing.

When I got to the barbershop, the floor had already been swept. In fact, it looked like Mr. Bobby was ready to pull the shades down, turn off the lights and leave.

"Hey, I've been waiting for you." Mr. Bobby greeted me at the door.

"How's it going, Mr. Bobby, am I late? It looks like you already cleaned the shop."

"No, son, you are right on time. I want to show you something. He unsnapped his smock to show me what was underneath: a shinning gold and red boxing championship belt.

"Wow! Mr. Bobby, where did you get that?" I was awestruck by the belt.

"I used to be a lightweight boxing champion. I started boxing in the military, the same place I learned to cut hair. I asked you to come here today to help you prepare for your big fight on Friday."

"Who told you about the fight, Mr. Bobby?"

Mr. Bobby did not answer directly. He only said, "Lots of people come to my barbershop and I hear lots of things… But I don't want to spend too much time talking; I have lots to teach you in a short period of time. You need to change into some shorts."

He handed me a pair of shorts, and then asked me to follow him into a back room. We entered a door that I had never noticed. The door was hidden behind posters and pictures of different haircut styles. When we got to the room behind the door, my jaw dropped. It was a small boxing gym, with a boxing ring and punching bag. It looked like a small training gym for boxers.

"Mr. Bobby, where did all of this come from?"

Mr. Bobby put his finger to his lips as if to say, *"Hush, this is our secret.* When I was your age, I was tall and gangly like you and people liked to pick on me, but I found that often, people's bite is not as loud as their bark and that their talk is cheap. Nowadays, these kids are cowards and want to use weapons. When I was a kid we would have to fight it out the old fashioned way, with our fists. And that is what I am going to teach you. This Barlow kid is a punk!" Mr. Bobby seemed angry. "He steals, starts fights and terrorizes people, and he will keep doing it until someone stops him. If he were as tough as he wants people to think he is, he would not hide and sneak. But don't worry, because come Friday you'll be ready for him."

Mr. Bobby wrapped my hands with bandage, then changed his clothes and put on his boxing shoes. He put on a pair of boxing gloves and gave me a pair.

Then he began teaching me boxing moves. By the time three hours of boxing training was over, I knew how to weave, block, punch, counterpunch, jab, uppercut and hook. When Mr. Bobby called an end to the boxing lesson, both he and I were sweating bullets.

Mr. Bobby did not cut me any slack while in the ring. He was really tough. He was 'in it to win it,' and to teach me how to win. I was relieved when Mr. Bobby said he'd give me a ride home, because my legs were too wobbly to walk. He'd given me lots of good advice and shared lots of wisdom. Just before I got out of the car, Mr. Bobby handed me a $20.00 bill.

"What's this for, Mr. Bobby?"

"Because I told your mother I would pay you."
"But I didn't do any work."

Mr. Bobby winked and said, "Whether or not you realize it, you just worked your behind off for the last three hours; you have the sweat to show for it and tomorrow you'll be nice and sore. Believe me son; you've earned that $20.00."

I thought about it and decided that Mr. Bobby was right and had a point, so I took the money. I told Mr. B, "thank you" and got out of the car.

CHAPTER 10

Wednesday was gym day. Boys and girls would be competing against one another in various exercises, we were all paired based on height and weight. The last event would decide the winner, either the boys or the girls. The members of the winning team would receive a book of coupons for treats at Gji's Sweet Shoppe.

We were now at the final event and the boys and girls were tied. It was all on Barlow to win it for the boys and the pressure was on. Mr. Steptoe, the gym teacher, Mr. Dane, the school engineer, and Mrs.

Princeton, my homeroom teacher, were judging the contest.

The final event was between Barlow and a girl in my class named Flossie Sims; and she was going to be hard to beat. She was the tallest and fastest girl in school.

For the final task, they each had to do 20 crunches, 20 push-ups, 20 pull-ups, run through an obstacle course to the other end of the gym, and then climb to the top of the rock-climbing wall. Everyone was on pins and needles. The boys were cheering for the boys and the girls were cheering for the girls.

Mr. Steptoe, the gym teacher, said, "Ready, set…" and blew his whistle for 'go.' Flossie moved so fast that it seemed she had a lead on Barlow. Although Flossie was ahead for push-ups and sit-ups and their time was pretty much tied, she tripped and fell running through the obstacle course, giving Barlow a slight lead.

They approached the climbing wall at the same time. She and Barlow were 'neck and neck' again. Everyone was cheering for his or her team! We were all cheering and jumping up and down. Ms. Jonsey, the cafeteria aide, was videotaping the race.

Flossie and Barlow were both approaching the top of the wall. When Mr. Steptoe blew his whistle, Flossie was closer to the top and was declared the winner!

The girls were jumping and screaming! Flossie did a great job! The guys in my class were disappointed to lose, but we all walked over to congratulate the girls, as a show of good sportsmanship. Well, almost everyone. Barlow did not go over; he was too busy sulking and stomping. When Xavier attempted to walk over and congratulate he girls, Barlow blocked him, not allowing him to cross. When Xavier attempted to clap for the girls, Barlow gave him a dirty look and Xavier stopped clapping.

Barlow was steaming mad, now! Without opening his mouth, Barlow motioned for Xavier to pick up both of their gym bags and carry them out of the gym. Xavier did as he was ordered. The two of them exited the gym without congratulating the winning team.

*****

All the girls in class were rallying around Flossie, when Ms. Jonsey noticed that Flossie did not look well.

It appeared that she was having an asthma attack. I heard Mrs. Princeton yell out, "Someone, look in Flossie's gym bag and bring her asthma inhaler, quick!"

Adam was standing near the wall where we had hung our gym bags, but did not see the one with Flossie's name on it. Everyone in class knew that Flossie kept her asthma medicine in her gym bag and if she did not get medicine soon, it could be dangerous for her.

This worried me. My cousin, Jahari has asthma, so I know how dangerous this condition can be. I looked out into the hallway and saw Lafi. I yelled out for Lafi to run and tell the school nurse to bring an inhaler for Flossie. Lafi took off running.

Mrs. Princeton had Flossie sit down on the gym floor and reminded her to stay calm. Mr. Dane explained to the students, who were looking on, that asthma is a condition that makes it hard to breathe.

The wait for the inhaler seemed like forever, but finally, the school nurse burst through the gymnasium doors, running towards Flossie with the inhaler in her hand.

I was exasperated. I said to Adam, "I know Barlow took her bag. I have to tell Mrs. Princeton what's going on."

"What if the kids in the class label you a snitch?" Adam asked.

"I don't care," I shrugged. "Barlow did not care when he took Flossie's bag with her medicine in it. And even if her medicine wasn't in it, he had no reason to touch her bag."

After school, I stayed behind. Lafi, Marie and Adam waited for me on the school steps. I went up to Mrs. Princeton's desk and told her of my suspicions.

"Do you have any proof that Barlow did this?" Mrs. Princeton was very serious and listened attentively.

"No, I don't. But I just know it's him. I just know it."

"Foster, I appreciate your concern, but this is a serious allegation for you to make and not have any proof; not to mention that you did not see Barlow take Flossie's bag, break into the art supply cabinet, write graffiti on the wall, go into the lockers or lunch bags of your classmates. These are serious charges, Foster."

"Sometimes, you just know it," I pleaded, "He's just bad news. Haven't you noticed how all of these strange things have only happened since he transferred here? Why, he was even kicked out of his last school for…"

"Foster, I have heard enough and I don't want to hear anymore of this. I appreciate your concern for Flossie's well being, but blaming and accusing your classmate for this type of devilment, especially without proof, is not fair."

"Ask Xavier. He'll tell you. He knows Barlow took the bag," I begged.

Mrs. Princeton waved her hands to stop me. "Tomorrow, let's see what we find out. I will ask the class if any one knows what happened to Flossie's gym bag. Okay?" But before I could answer, she told me good-bye and to have a good evening.

*****

"What happened?" asked Adam.

"Yeah, what did your teacher say?" Lafi wanted to know.

"Yeah, what did she say?" Marie repeated.

"She didn't believe me. She said if I had no proof, there was nothing she could do. I even told her to ask Xavier and she shook her head, *no*."

Marie got mad, thinking about Mrs. Princeton not believing Foster. Anyone who knew Foster knew that he was no liar. The teacher should have believed him. Then, Marie blurted out, "Foster, when you and Barlow fight on Friday, let him have it between the ears… punch him in the sockets. I mean let him have *it* and let him have *it* good." Marie was talking through gritted teeth, and swinging her arms and fist in a furious fit!

I liked all the confidence Marie had in me and I was surprised by it. I had to figure out a way to catch Barlow in the act, before he caused real damage and someone was seriously hurt.

As Marie, Lafi, Adam and I walked home, three fast moving police cars passed us with their sirens and lights on. They were headed in the direction of the school. Lafi joked, "Maybe they are going to get Barlow."

CHAPTER 11

By Thursday, things were really bad. With the exception of the fight that Barlow and I were expected to have, I could not imagine things getting much worse. But they did. I am not sure what was going on at school, but something was happening. All the teachers were acting strangely.

After Mrs. Princeton took attendance, the principal came and asked her to please meet her in the hallway to talk for a moment. Mrs. Princeton came back into the classroom, checked on us and gave us 10 practice math problems to work on. Then she went back in the hall to talk to Mr. Steptoe, Mr. Dane and Ms. Jonsey and the school nurse. They were all huddled together discussing something serious.

I had finished my math problems when I noticed Xavier get up and walk over to the pencil sharpener, near the window. I got up, walked over to him and said, "Xavier, you know yesterday after you and Barlow left the gym, Flossie had an asthma attack and no one could find her gym bag. If you know anything about what happened to it, you should say something."

"Man, I don't know what you're talking about," Xavier said. But I could tell he wasn't telling the truth, because he did not look me in the eye when he talked to me.

I replied, "All I'm saying is, if they find out you were involved, you're going to be in a lot of trouble."

"You better shut-up! YOU ain't sayin' nothing," Barlow interrupted. "If you have something to say to "X," then you best say it to me. Can you dig?"

"So, it's like that, Xavier? Or should I call you, X? You cannot speak or think for yourself... You let Barlow tell you who you can and cannot talk to?"

My classmates were all looking up and beginning to whisper. Mrs. Princeton must have heard something, too, because she came into the room. "Simmer down, class! Why are the three of you over here at the pencil sharper? Go and take your seats!" she commanded.

Barlow was the last to sit down. He made sure to make eye contact with me, then breaking three of his pencils one by one, while starring at me. I guess he was trying to scare me, but I just smiled at him. I had no fear. I was ready for him.

Mrs. Princeton must have wanted to keep us busy, because she gave us ten more math problems, plus ten words to look up the definitions for. But this time, when she went in the hall, they were talking much louder and Rosey Dominquez, or 'nosy Rosey,' as we call her, planted her ear up to the door, listened and then repeated everything she heard the teachers talking about in the hall…

"Wow!" she belted out. "It looks like yesterday, after school, somebody vandalized Mrs. Princeton, Mr. Steptoe, and Mr. Dane's cars, in the parking lot. Someone took the air out of their tires, broke their windows, and painted and wrote on their cars."

"Ah, man!" "No way!" and "For real?" was all you could hear from the students in my class.

Just then Adam and Foster remembered hearing the police sirens yesterday.

Adam and I looked at each other, and then we look at Barlow. We could not imagine that he would be so bold and stupid as to tamper with the teacher's cars, so we dismissed that thought. Then Mrs. Princeton returned to the classroom and asked us to put our books away and get ready for the spelling test.

Mrs. Princeton would not begin any test unless all the students were in their seats. And so, we sat quietly waiting for Dana, who sits in front of me, to return from the washroom. When she got back to the classroom, she said, "Xavier, I just saw your mom walking in the hallway."

"My momma? My momma!" Xavier jumped up. He had been resting his head on his desk. Now he couldn't keep still. He seemed nervous and his eyes were welling up with tears. "What's my momma doing up here?"

A few minutes later, the principal came into the class. "Excuse me," she said, "Xavier Peoples, please gather your belongings and come with me."

Xavier looked around as if he could not figure out whom she was talking to, but she pointed at him and said, "I am talking to you." She was not smiling. Xavier looked back at Barlow as he went out the door and towards the principal's office, but Barlow just looked away. I figured that Xavier took the blame for taking Flossie's gym bag… *But how did they find out? I* wondered. There was no proof…

Minutes later, we saw Xavier walking pass the classroom with his mom, he was walking toward the school exit. He was crying and dragging his book bag. We could hear his mom fussing at him and then she popped him on the back of his head. She was obviously angry. They left the building. Mrs. Princeton did not say a word, but just shook her head. And this was all before lunch!

On the playground, Barlow looked lost and lonely without Xavier, his sidekick. *He didn't have anyone to boss around.* Adam, Lafi and I watched as he walked up to several groups of people on the playground, but they either turned their backs to him or just walked away from him. Our classmates had begun to sense that he was a troublemaker and did not welcome his company.

As we were lining up to go back into the classroom, we saw three police cars pulling up in front of the school.

"What do you think happened now?' Lafi asked. "I don't know. I don't even want to know," I said and Adam agreed.

*****

Things got really wacky after lunch and recess. After we got back inside the classroom, we were informed that police officers were in the school looking for something and that we should not be distracted. But, of course we were, since we were not used to seeing police in school.

Next, the principal came back to my classroom and asked Barlow to please come with her and bring his belongings. Barlow didn't move. He just stared at her, as if he hadn't heard her speak. "Now!" she demanded.

"Adam, will you please take your seat," said Mrs.

Princeton.

"I am in my seat, ma'am," Adam was already sitting, so he did not understand what she was saying.

"No, I mean take your seat in the back of the class. Barlow Darden will not be returning," she said simply and offered no other explanation.

"Hey look," Loxie yelled out as she pointed outside the window. The entire class ran to the window and watched in amazement as Barlow walked in handcuffs to the police car with an officer.

CHAPTER 12

Since Barlow had been removed from the school, there was no fight on Friday, but there was an assembly Friday afternoon. A police officer and a school counselor were the guest speakers. The assembly was about bullying and violence in school. The principal went over the student handbook and read the rules about bullying, violence, hate crimes, misconduct, stealing, fighting and weapons in school. She also read the school's discipline policy. The counselor explained that a person does not have to hit you or even put their hands on you to be a bully. She reminded us that every student has a right to receive an education in a safe environment. The officer encouraged students not be afraid of being called a 'snitch, but instead to report any and all misconduct to an adult. We saw a film on bullying and the consequences of bullying.

Before the assembly, nosey-Rosey told a group of us what happened with Barlow…

Coincidentally, without knowing it, while Ms. Jonsey filmed the Olympic competition in gym class, she had also taped Barlow picking up Flossie's gym bag and handing it over to Xavier. This happened while the girls were jumping up and down and they were celebrating their big win. Xavier did not want to take the bag, but Barlow forced him to take it. Then the two of them left the gym. Xavier had been suspended from school for one week, for not only being an accomplice, but also for not reporting Barlow.

When Flossie started to have an asthma attack, Ms. Jonsey sat her video recorder on the window seal so that she could assist with Flossie until the school nurse arrived. Apparently with all of the commotion Ms. Jonsey forgot to turn the camera off. The camera lens was facing outside the window and it filmed Barlow in an angry fit vandalizing Mrs. Princeton, Mr. Steptoe and Mr. Dane's cars. He was upset that they had judged the contest and declared Flossie the winner, so he thought he'd get even with them by letting the air out of the teachers' tires, busting the windows out, and spray painting the cars and scratching the sides of their cars with his keys.

Barlow was expelled from our school, which meant he could not ever return. No one knew what was going to happen to him, other than he was being charged as a criminal for vandalizing property and theft. Ms. Jonsey had no idea she had taped all of this. But the police said it was all evidence to use against him in court. Later that day when the principal and Mrs. Princeton checked his locker they found money, juice boxes, a stash of missing lunches, art supplies, a box-cutter with a sharp blade, and Flossie's asthma inhaler.

"Wow!" Lafi said. "Unbelievable" Adam said. "Finally, there was proof," I said.

Marie chimed in, "He's lucky the police got him before my brother, cause Foster would have made him *'hurt like the dickens'*... with a big 'gotcha-gotcha' on top of his big head."

We all laughed at Marie, but we also felt bad about the situation.

After the dismissal bell rang, Mrs. Princeton called me up to her desk. "Foster, I am sorry that I did not listen to you. It turns out that you were right about everything. If anything ever happens that you notice or observe, please come and talk to me, I promise to listen.

"Deal," I told her, "I'm looking forward to getting things back to normal around here."

And by the way, Mr. Dane is going to clean out your locker over the weekend and you'll be happy to know that you will have the locker to yourself for the remainder of the school year."

"YES!" I shouted, pumping my fist in the air.

*****

That evening at home, Marie and I told our parents everything.

"I cannot believe that you two did not say anything before today," my mother said. I could tell she was ticked-off.

"Mom, I knew you would either worry or call the school, and I could handle it," I tried to explain.

"Your mom is right," my father said, "It sounds like this kid has some serious issues and problems, and you really don't know if this was something you would have been able to deal with on your own. You should have told an adult."

"I tried, but Mrs. Princeton wouldn't listen." "Well, next time, you tell a different adult, and if that one does not listen, you tell another and another and another… do you understand? And know that you can always come to us, your parents," my mom continued.

"I understand," I said. "I do, too," said Marie.

"But I was ready for him," I boasted. I got up from the table and started to show my parents the moves I learned from watching the Kung-Fu movies, and from Mr. Bobby. I shadow danced, doing my fancy boxing footwork, did a jab and a punch then combined it with a karate kick. *I really thought I was doing something...* Then I heard my pants rip up the back... My Mom, Dad and Marie laughed as I danced my way out of the kitchen trying to hide the big hole in back of my pants.

The End

QUESTIONS FOR THOUGHT & DISCUSSION

1. Why do you think Barlow tried to take the tickets away from Foster and his friends?
2. Why didn't the students in Kevin's class want to 'snitch' when Barlow was doing mean and harassing things to them? What would you have done?
3. When Foster and his friends were at The Maxx Extreme Sports Park, they ordered lots of foods, because there weren't any adults around to stop them. What foods would you order if you had an opportunity?
4. Has anyone ever bullied you or a friend or family member? How did you (they) handle it?
5. If you tried to tell an adult that a student was bullying or stealing, and the adult did not listen to you, what would you do?

Ask your teacher to show you and your class the rules of the school, the Student Bill of Rights, and the disciplinary code.

Think of additional rules that you and your class can write to help respect and improve the environment of your classroom.

Think of a project, maybe art or poetry, that your class can do to promote 'no violence' and unity for all. Then ask your teacher if you can display your artistic 'peace' pieces throughout the school and community.

ABOUT THE AUTHOR

Jil Ross   *Photo by Walter Mitchell*

Jil Ross began writing when her children were little, while recuperating from a broken leg. As the children got older, she wrote about the various antics and mischief they got themselves into. Her children are the inspiration for many of her writings. She resides in Chicago, IL, with her family.

What They Are Saying About Jil Ross & the *Shenanigans Series*™

"The kids who read her books relate to what the stories are about."

— Chicago Sun-Times

"Ross thinks parents need to be more invested in their children and more mindful of the types of messages they are exposed to. She hopes her books will lead to discussions of the important issues parents and children might normally avoid talking about."

— Catholic Herald

"Although the Shenanigans Series are humorous and entertaining, they also teach clear, but gently told life lessons."

— Diversity MBA Magazine

"This is an area that particularly inner-city schools seem to be interested in."

— Chicago Tribune

www.ingramcontent.com/pod-product-compliance
Lightning Source LLC
Chambersburg PA
CBHW060948040426
42445CB00011B/1058